A Dog's Book of Bugs

A Dog's Book of Bugs

Text by Elizabeth Griffen

Drawings by Peter Parnall

AN ALADDIN BOOK
Atheneum

PUBLISHED BY ATHENEUM

PUBLISHED SIMULTANEOUSLY IN CANADA BY
MCCLELLAND & STEWART LTD.
MANUFACTURED IN THE UNITED STATES OF AMERICA BY
CONNECTICUT PRINTERS, INC., BLOOMFIELD, CONN.
ISBN 0-689-70408-9
FIRST ALADDIN EDITION

DEDICATED
with affection
to four generations of a family
that has delighted in bugs:
Jo-Jo and Mickey
Gruffy
Rosie
Emily

FOR DOGS ONLY

This book is for dogs that like bugs.

Not all dogs have discovered the buzzing, bumbling, leaping, creeping world of bugs.

But many have.

They search out the ways of bugs with curiosity,

with patience,

and with joy.

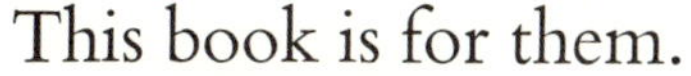

This book is for them.

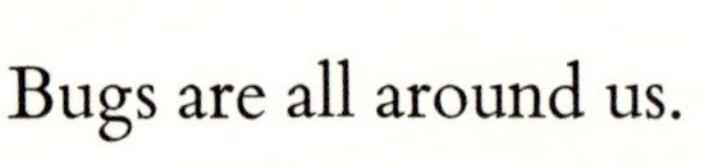

Bugs are all around us.

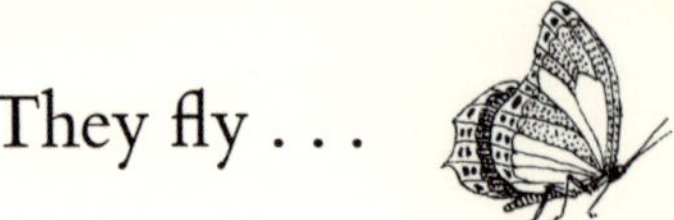

They fly . . .

They're small. They crawl on anything at all. They . . . fall.

They burrow in the bark of logs and scurry in the hair of dogs.

They tunnel down in earthy places, digging different kinds of spaces.

. . . by.

They zip and zoom where flowers bloom.

On streams they skate and skim and swim.

They hop and leap into the air.

They stop and sleep anywhere.

They cling to things.

They climb all the time.

Bugs are easy to find.

Here, for instance, is . . .

. . . something going somewhere in a hurry.

It smells interesting, but it tastes rather hot.

Now it has . . .

. . . disappeared. Where did it go?

ANT

Sometimes ants have wings.

Ants live together.

They work together.

It flies into blossoms
and clambers out.

Something buzzy is busy in the flowers.

It's finding food.
It eats some
and takes some home.

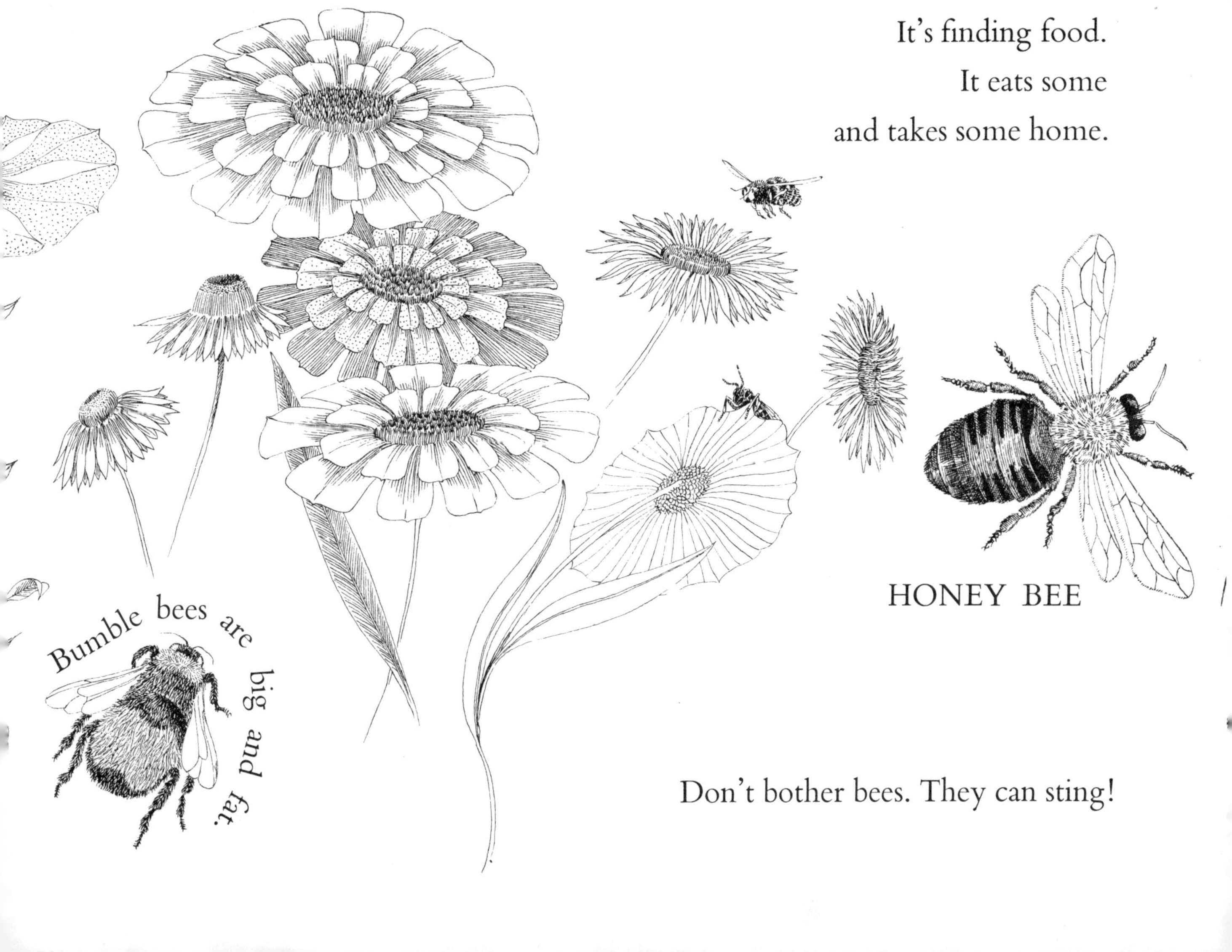

Bumble bees are big and fat.

HONEY BEE

Don't bother bees. They can sting!

Can these sting, too?

Yes! Look out!

WASP

They sting like this:

Here comes something small and spotted.
It seems quite friendly.

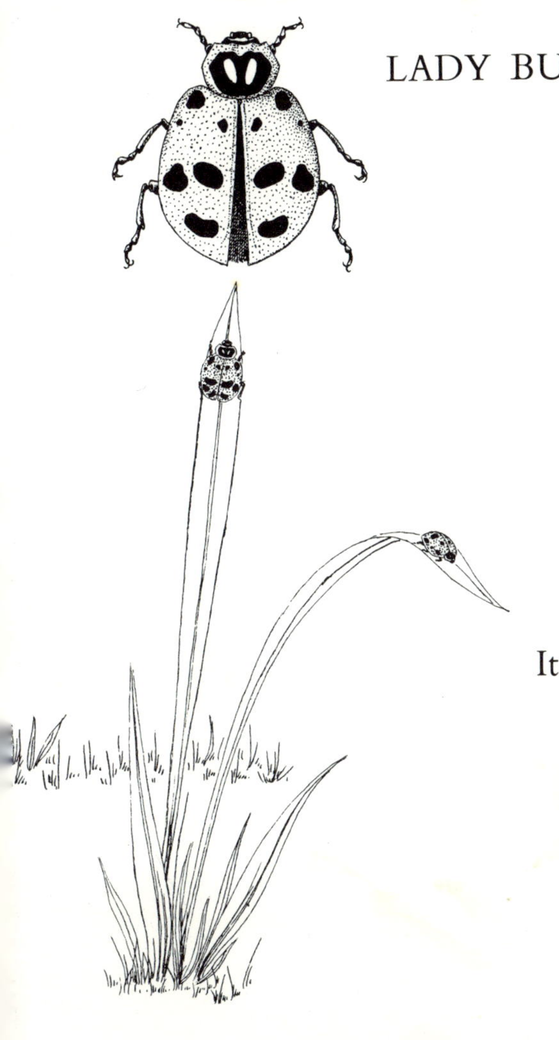

LADY BUG

It's not afraid to walk on your paw.

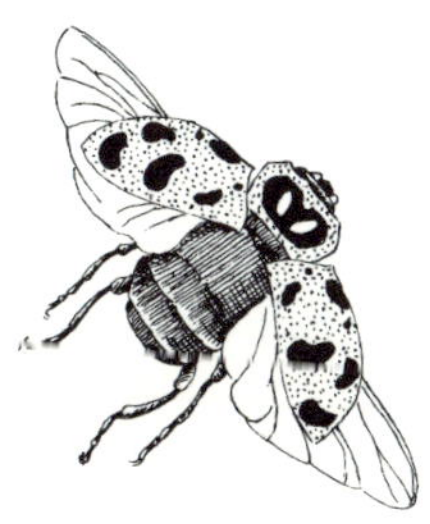

It can fly away.

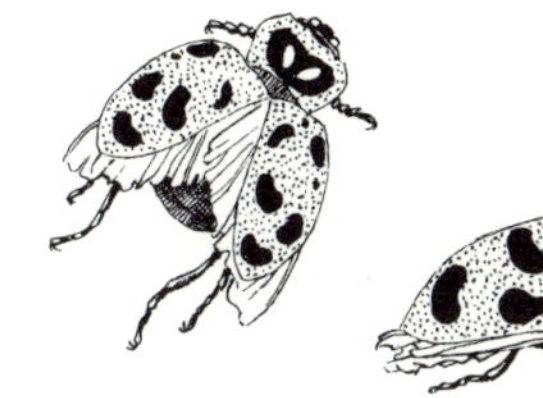

Sometimes it leaves its underthings hanging out.

Some bugs bump into things when they fly.
Dogs play jumping games with them.

JUNE BUG

LIGHTNING BUG

Some bugs carry their own lights.

Some bugs pinch.

PINCHING BUG

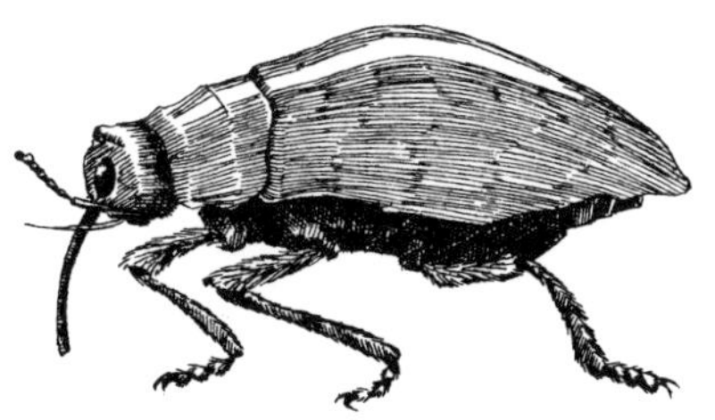

SNOUT BEETLE

They're rather small.
Many dogs don't notice them at all.

Some have snouts.

Some bugs live in very interesting places.

GROUND BEETLE

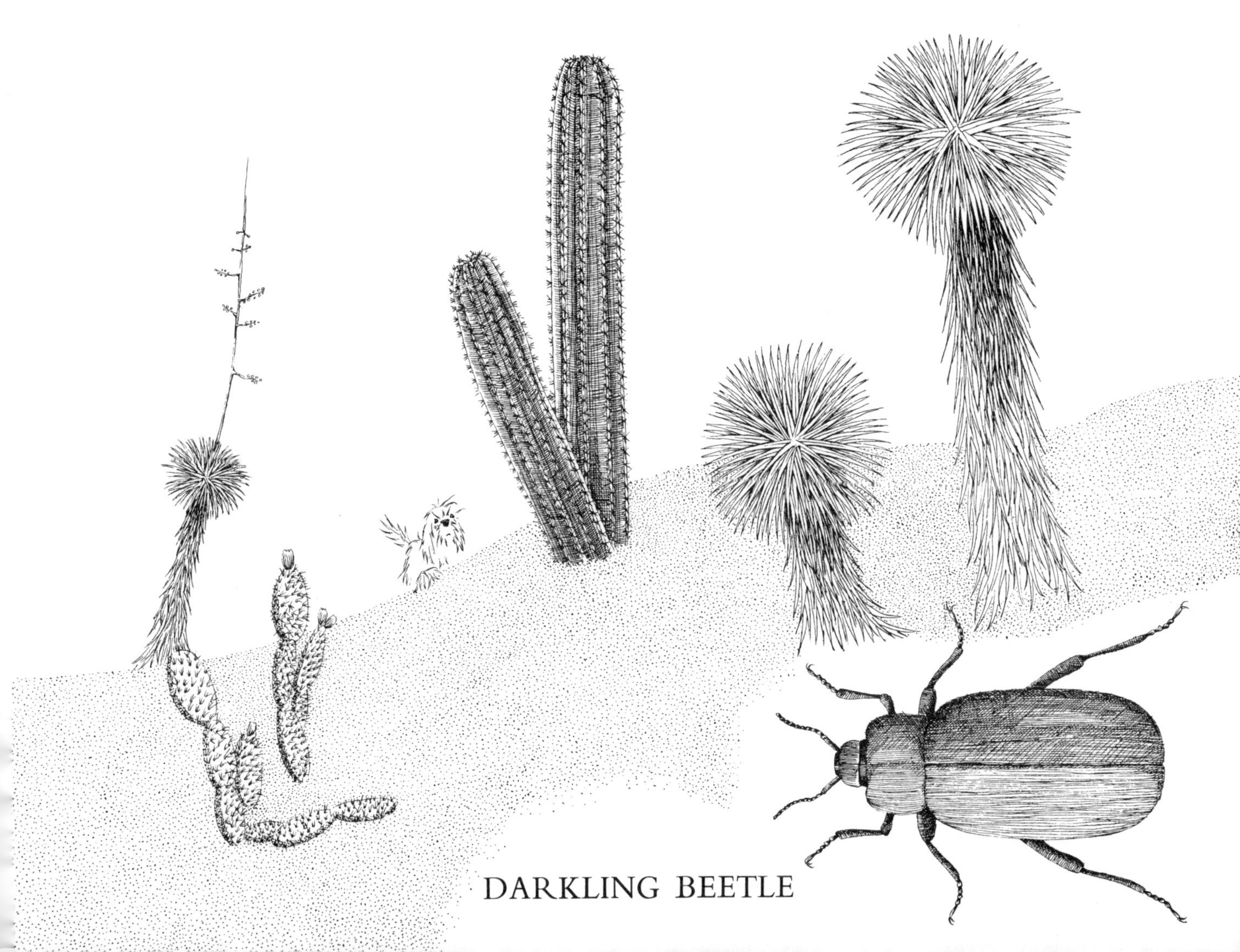

DARKLING BEETLE

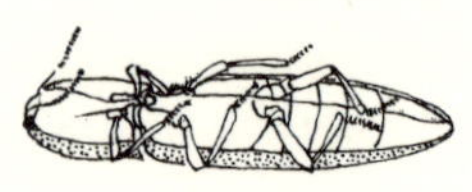

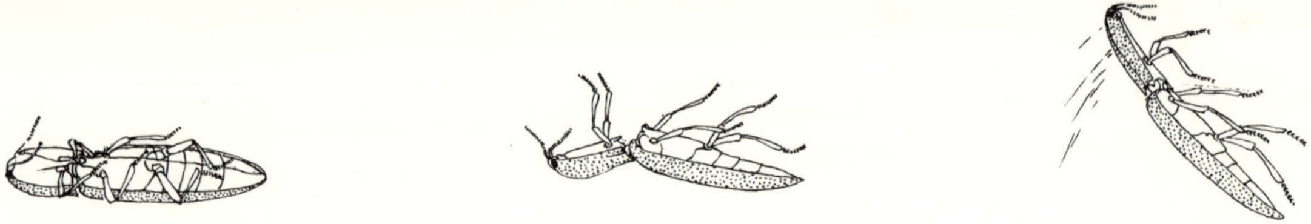

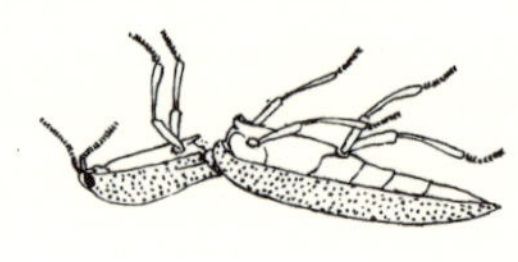

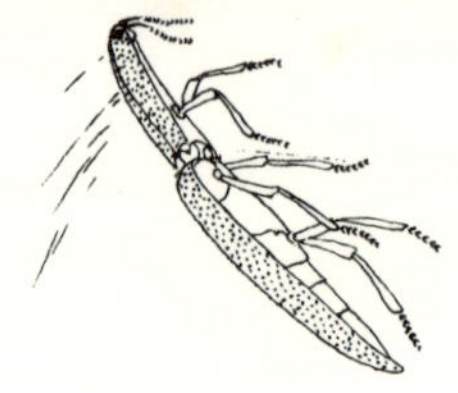

A bug on its back?

Click! It shoots up,

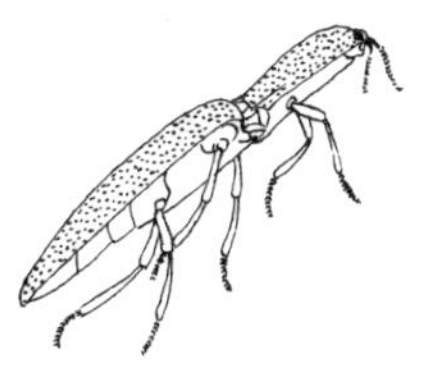

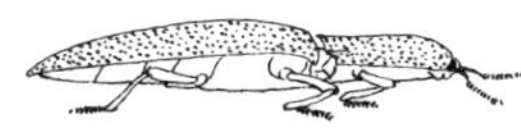

turns end over end,

lands right side up,

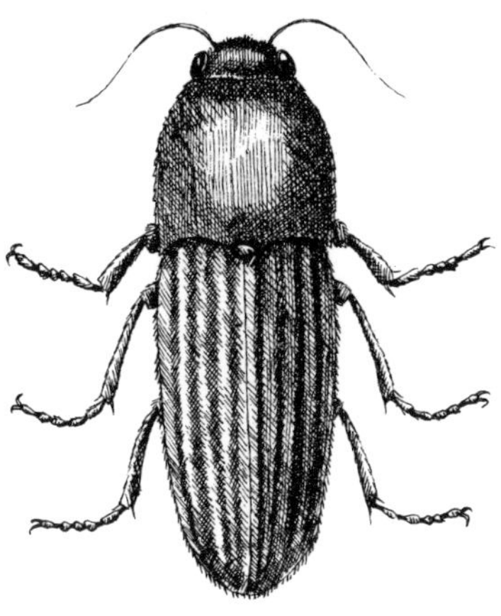

CLICK BEETLE

and hurries off . . .

Flies come in different sizes.

Some are buzzy and bothersome.

HOUSE FLY

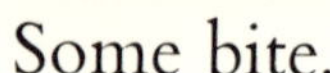

Some bite.

BLACK FLY

DEER FLY

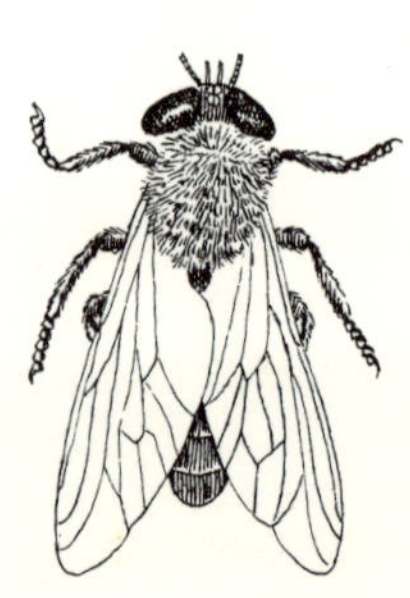

HORSE FLY
(It's really as big as this.)

NO-SEE-UM

GNAT

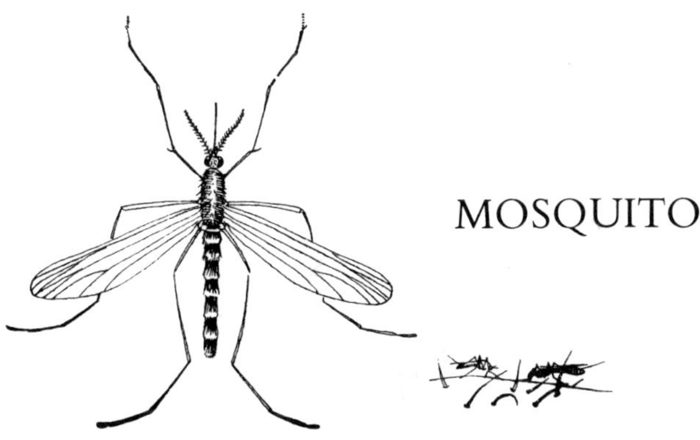

MOSQUITO

Some don't bother anyone.

CRANE FLY
(It's this big.)

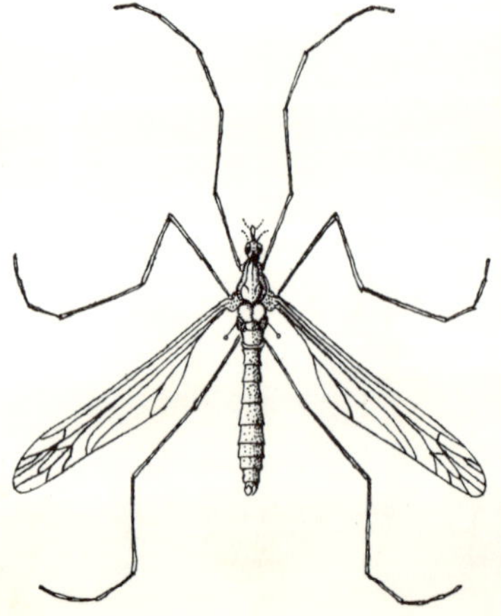

Some fly round and round.
Don't they *ever* come down?

HOVER FLY

In the grass, something is hopping with great big hops.
Stop, hopper!

Oops! It got away!

What *was* it?

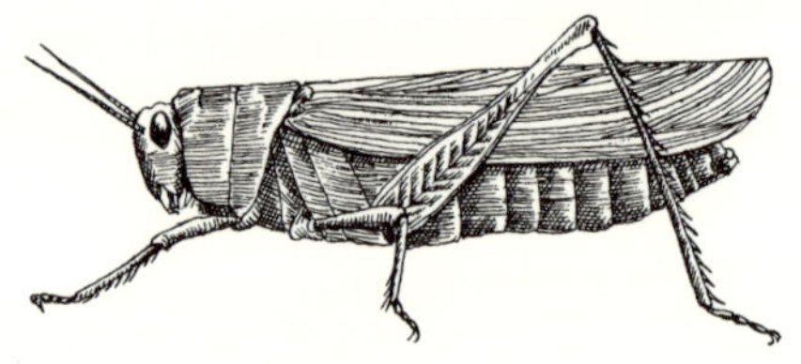

GRASSHOPPER

It has long, strong jumping legs.

It may have colored wings.

In the evening, the trees and bushes are very noisy.

Is it an argument?

Katy *did*!
Katy *did*n't!
Katy did, did, did.

KATYDID

But there is no one to be seen.

Here's another jumper!

Be quick!

Catch it!

Where did it go?

From its hiding place,
it will sing with its wings.

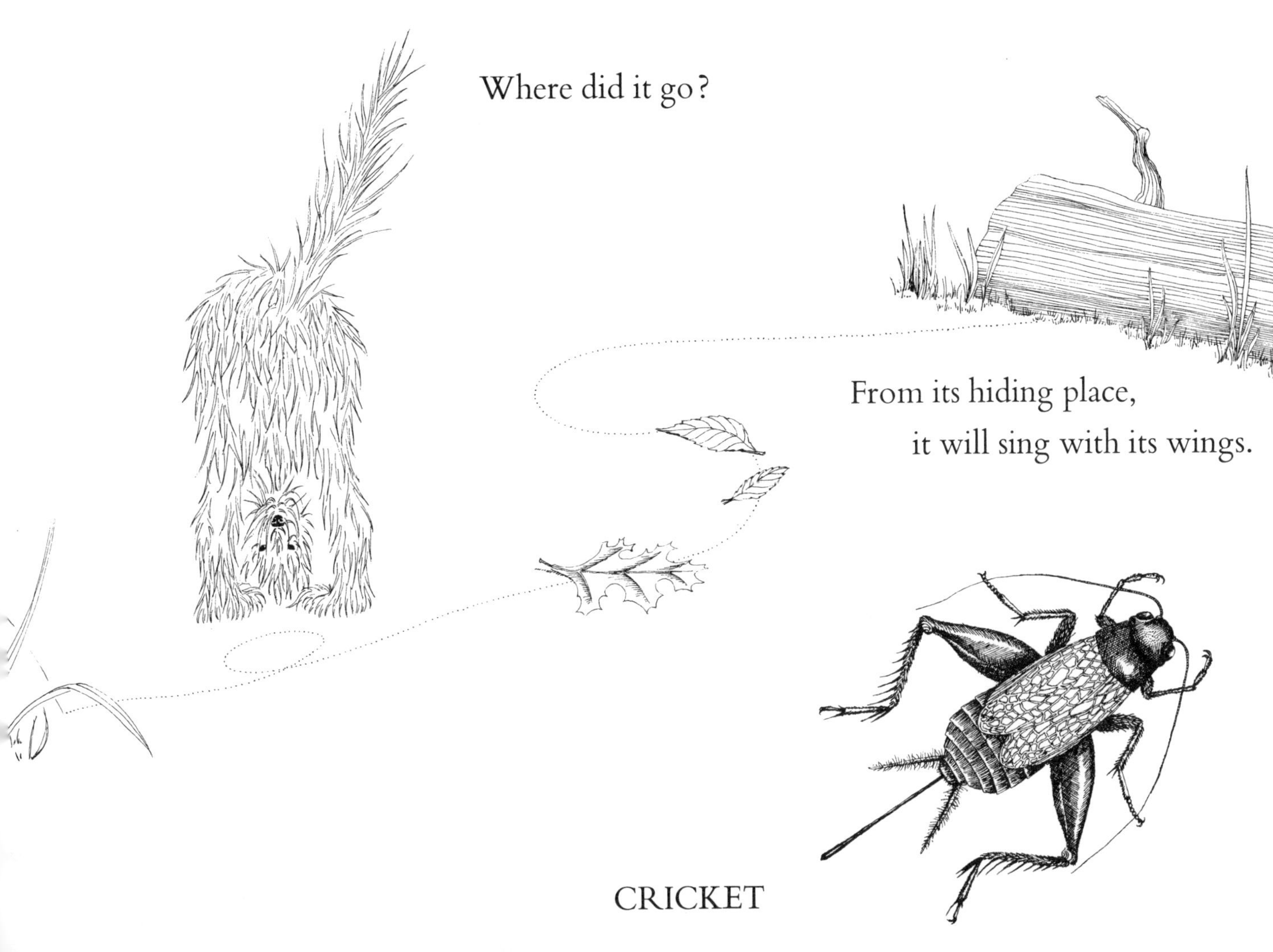

CRICKET

This stick seems to be walking.

It moves very slowly.

WALKING STICK

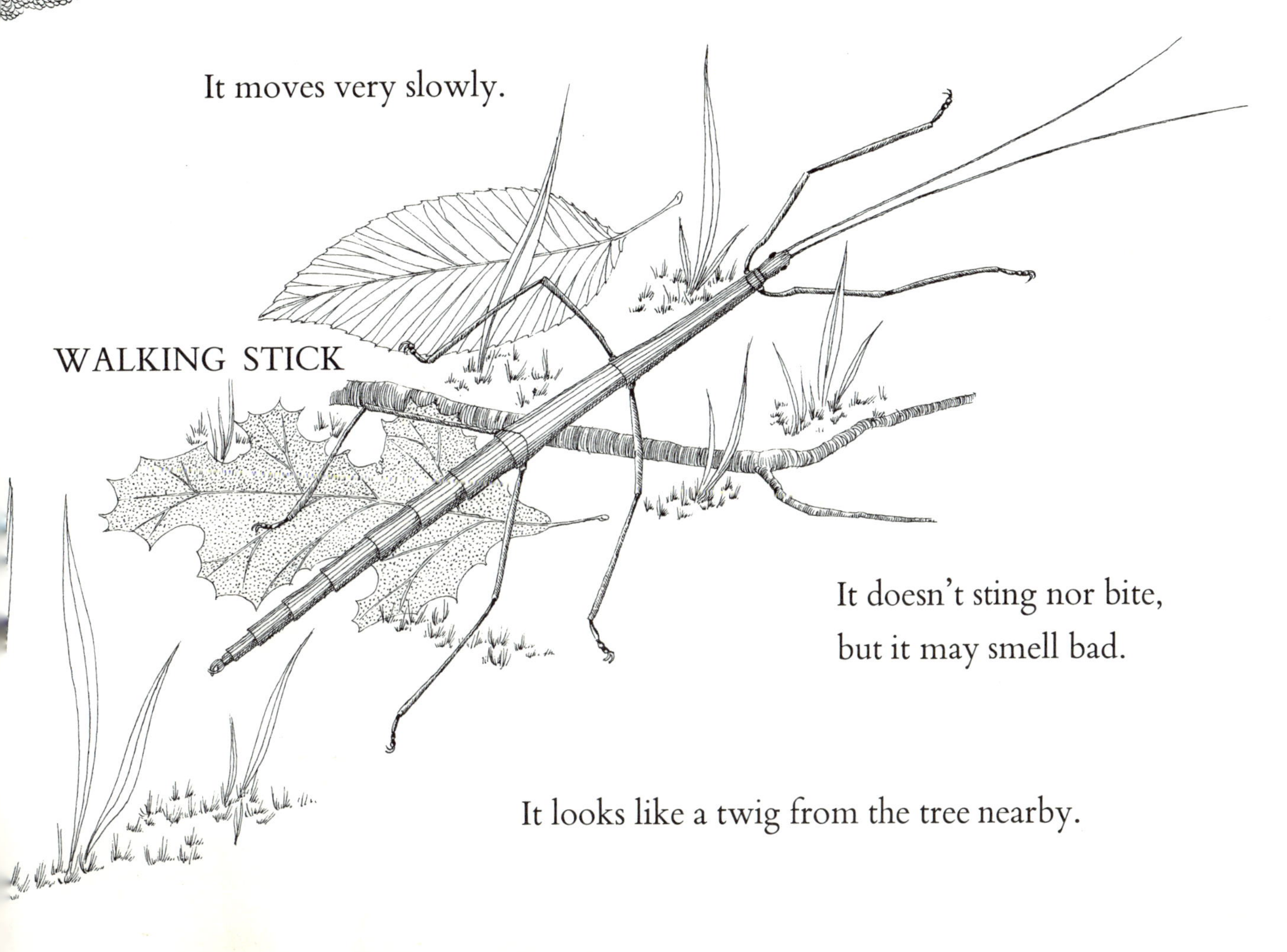

It doesn't sting nor bite,
but it may smell bad.

It looks like a twig from the tree nearby.

Something just ran across the floor.

What was it?

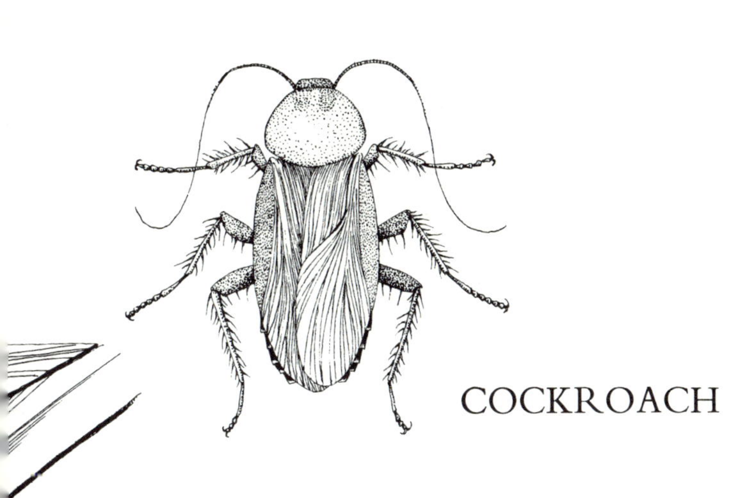

COCKROACH

It comes out at night.

It has long sweeping feelers, but its head is hidden.

Nobody likes it in the house.

Some bugs are pests.

They live in fur and feathers.

FLEA

They have jumping legs, but no wings.

They bite!

Some bugs smell bad and taste worse. Ugh!

TREEHOPPER

Is it a thorn, or is it a bug?
If it hops, it's not a thorn.

Some bugs live on the water.

WATER SKATER

It skates on top of the water.

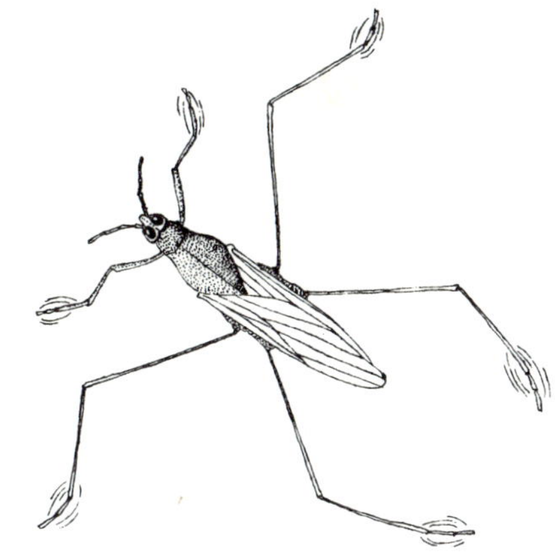

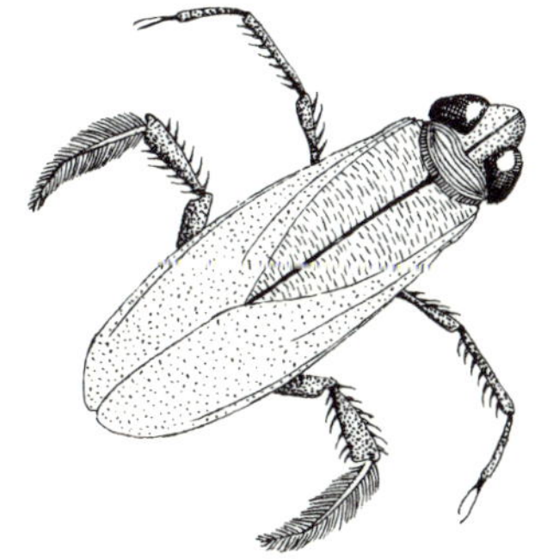

WATER BOATMAN

It rows with its legs.

WHIRLIGIG BEETLE

It swims round and round in circles.

An empty bug?

No, an empty skin, left by something that flew up into the tree . . .

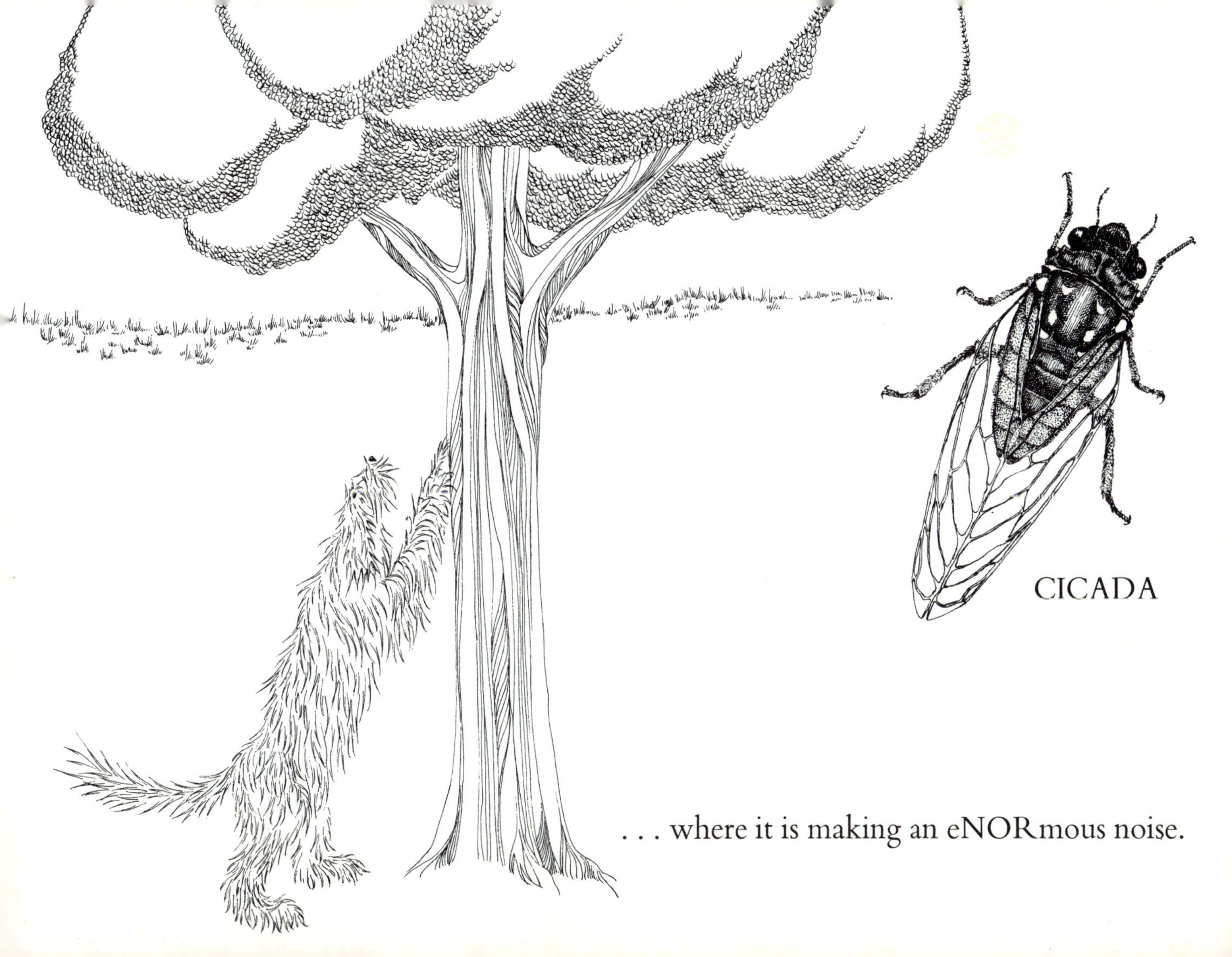

. . . where it is making an eNORmous noise.

Here in the meadow, there are blobs of wetness on the plant stems.

Each one is a damp little house
made by a young bug
that likes to be rather wet.

A SPIT BUG lives here.

When the young bug grows up,
it leaves its bubbly house
and hops away.

A bug in the bathtub?

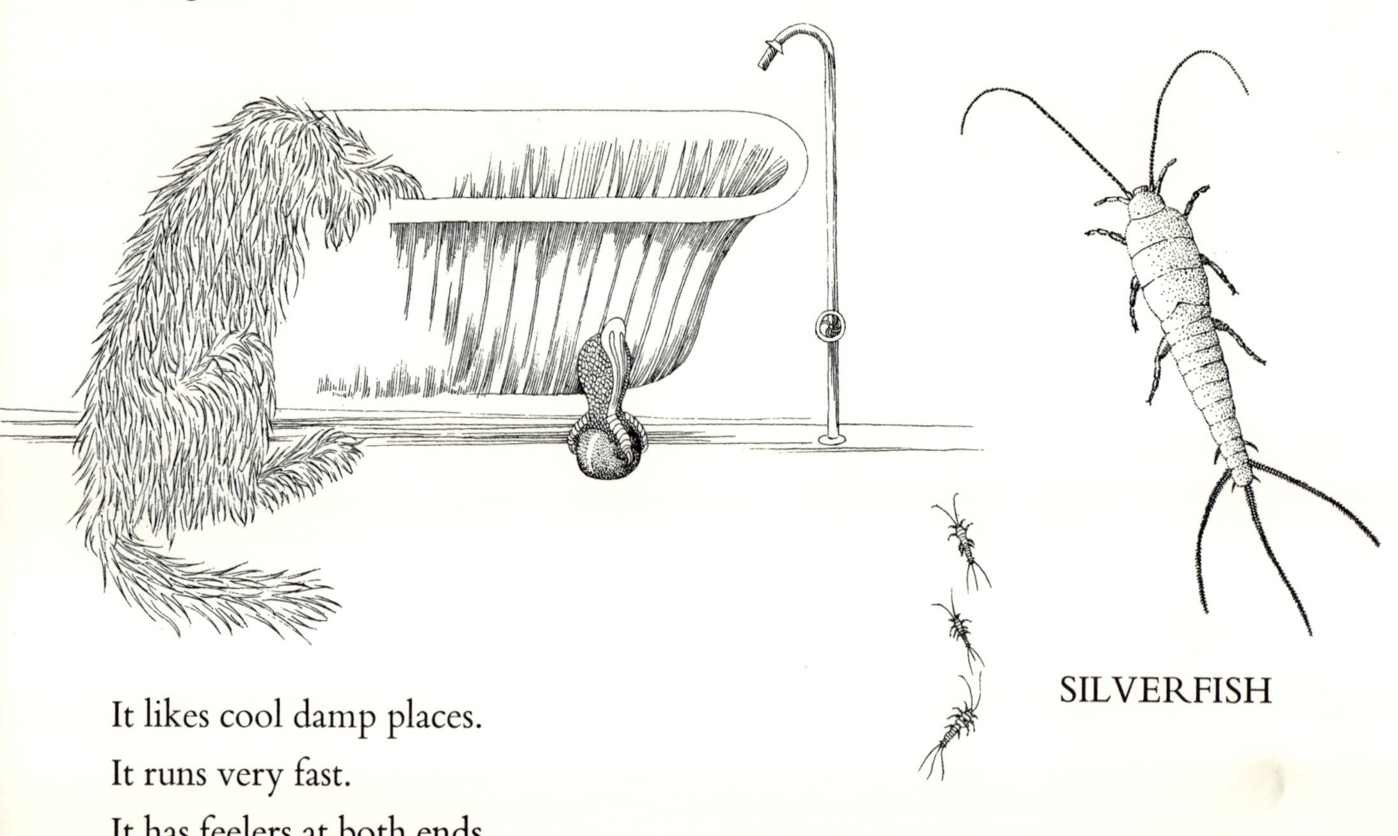

It likes cool damp places.
It runs very fast.
It has feelers at both ends.

SILVERFISH

If you ever meet a small something
with pinchers on its tail,
it's probably an . . .

EARWIG

It won't hurt you.

Look! By the brook,

something is glinting in the sunlight.

Zip! It's gone.

It looks like a kind of airplane.

DRAGONFLY

(Some are even bigger than this.)

It catches food while flying.

It doesn't sting nor bite.

In the summer sunshine, what flutters by?

Butterflies!

They suck nectar from flowers.

BUTTERFLY

MOTH

At night the moths come out . . .

. . . and dogs go in.